REAL WORLD DATA

GRAPHING WAR AND CONFLICT

Andrew Solway

Heinemann
LIBRARY

Chicago, Illinois

www.heinemannraintree.com
Visit our website to find out
more information about
Heinemann-Raintree books.

To order:

☎ Phone 888-454-2279

💻 Visit www.heinemannraintree.com
to browse our catalog and order online.

Edited by Megan Cotugno and Diyan Leake
Designed by Victoria Bevan and Geoff Ward
Original illustrations © Capstone Global Library, LLC 2010
Illustrated by Geoff Ward
Picture research by Ruth Blair, Zooid Pictures Ltd
Originated by Chroma Graphics (Overseas) Ltd
Printed in China by Leo Paper Products Ltd

14 13 12 11 10
10 9 8 7 6 5 4 3 2 1

Library of Congress Cataloging-in-Publication Data
Solway, Andrew.
  Graphing war and conflict / Andrew Solway. -- 1st ed.
    p. cm. -- (Real world data)
  Includes bibliographical references and index.
  ISBN 978-1-4329-2620-5 (hc) -- ISBN 978-1-4329-2629-
8 (pb) 1. Military history, Modern. 2. Military history,
Modern--Charts, diagrams, etc. 3. Military art and science--
History. 4. Military art and science--Charts, diagrams, etc. I.
Title.
  D214.S65 2009
  355.02--dc22
                              2009001188

Acknowledgments

The author and publishers are grateful to the following for
permission to reproduce copyright material: Corbis pp. **4**
(Atef Hassan/Reuters), **6** (Bettmann), **9** (Hulton-Deutsch
Collection), **14**, **16** (Bettmann), **18** (Badri Media/Epa), **20**
(Mohamed Messara/Epa), **25** (Hulton-Deutsch Collection), **26**
(Arko Datta/Reuters); Getty Images pp. **12** (Shah Marai/AFP),
23 (AFP); Lockheed Martin **10**.

Cover photograph of a U.S. soldier in Afghanistan
reproduced with permission of Getty Images (Darren
McCollester/Stringer).

We would like to thank Dr. John Allen Williams for his
invaluable help in the preparation of this book.

Every effort has been made to contact copyright holders
of any material reproduced in this book. Any omissions
will be rectified in subsequent printings if notice is given
to the publishers.

All the Internet addresses (URLs) given in this book were
valid at the time of going to press. However, due to the
dynamic nature of the Internet, some addresses may have
changed, or sites may have changed or ceased to exist since
publication. While the author and publishers regret any
inconvenience this may cause readers, no responsibility
for any such changes can be accepted by either the author
or the publishers.

CONTENTS

Some words are printed in bold, **like this**. You can find out what they mean by looking in the glossary, on page 30.

WAR AND PEACE

Human beings are social. They like living together in groups. Most of the time, people live together peacefully. But sometimes they come into **conflict**, or disagree with each other. When a disagreement cannot be resolved by talking, it can often lead to fighting. War is when a conflict between two or more countries, or within a country, leads to fighting.

Changing wars

The way that wars are fought has changed as technology (practical ways of using science) has changed. A thousand years ago, most wars were fought with weapons such as swords and spears. Even then, change was beginning to happen. In China, gunpowder was invented around 800 CE. It was used to make rocket-powered arrows and bombs thrown by catapults.

 Below, a heavily armed soldier stands guard in Iraq. The technology of war has changed drastically over the years.

The secret of gunpowder soon spread across Asia and into Europe. By the 14th century, European armies were firing at each other using cannons and guns. At first these weapons were not very powerful or accurate. But gradually the weapons improved, and they changed the way that wars were fought. Soldiers shot at each other from a distance instead of fighting hand to hand. Cannons became powerful enough to break through even the strongest walls. **Fortified** castles and towns became a thing of the past.

Graphs and charts

Graphs and charts show information, or data, visually. This helps us to see shapes or patterns in the data. The main types of graphs are bar graphs, pie charts, and line graphs. A line graph is especially good for showing how something changes over time. The graph below shows how world military spending has changed from 1992 to 2006.

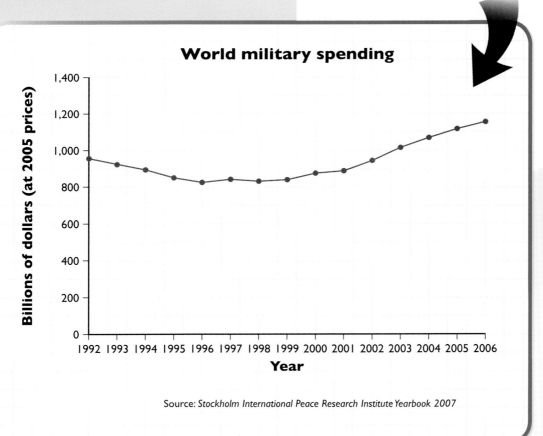

Source: *Stockholm International Peace Research Institute Yearbook 2007*

MOTORIZED WAR

In the 19th and early 20th centuries, there were big changes in the way that wars were fought. This was mainly because of improved guns and the development of motorized transportation. Trains, and later trucks, made it possible to move soldiers and large weapons more quickly from place to place. At sea, warships no longer relied on the wind to move from place to place. And the invention of aircraft led to warfare in the skies.

In World War I (1914–1918), tanks and aircraft were used in war for the first time. By World War II (1939–1945), wars had become much more complex and fast-moving. Tanks and trucks could move a whole **division** of troops many miles in a few hours. Aircraft could drop bombs or paratroopers deep in enemy territory. Long-distance communications became essential to planning and controlling what happened in a war.

Fooling submarines

During World War I, submarines were used in battles for the first time. German submarines (U-boats) caused huge amounts of damage by attacking and sinking merchant ships. To try to stop the U-boats, the British Navy developed Q-ships. These were small merchant ships with hidden guns. The ships were too small for U-boats to waste torpedoes on. Instead, the U-boats attacked on the surface. When they did, they got a big surprise as the Q-ships opened fire.

 U.S. paratroopers land on Indonesia during World War II. Indonesia was under Japanese control at the time.

Modern wars

Wars are fought for many reasons. A war may be over a disputed piece of land. It may begin because of differences in religion, race, or culture. It may be a dispute over supplies such as fuel (oil) or steel.

Since World War II, the kinds of wars that are fought have changed hugely. Large-scale battles between similar armies have been replaced by smaller-scale fights.

The boundaries between fighting troops and **civilians** are less clear than they were in the past. And technology such as jets, nuclear bombs, and missiles have made it possible for countries to fight wars against enemies who are thousands of miles away.

This book will look at how warfare has changed in recent times, and how fighting forces are adapting to these changes. It will use graphs and charts to help explain some ideas and to learn more about warfare.

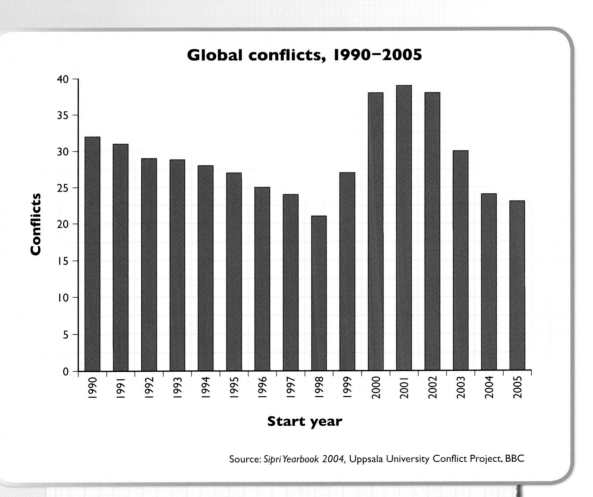

Global conflicts, 1990–2005

Source: *Sipri Yearbook 2004*, Uppsala University Conflict Project, BBC

This bar graph shows the number of major conflicts between 1990 and 2005. Although the number of conflicts rise and fall, there are always wars happening somewhere in the world.

CONVENTIONAL WARFARE

Conventional warfare is the way war has generally happened in the past. This is fighting between the **armed forces** of two or more countries. The aim is to destroy the enemy's army, or weaken the enemy so much that it surrenders.

Conventional wars in the past

In the past, conventional wars involved large battles, often away from major towns and cities. The main **casualties** in these battles were the fighters on each side. For example, in World War I most of the fighting happened along the Western Front. This was a 700-kilometer (440-mile) line of **trenches** and barbed wire that stretched across northern France and Belgium. There were not many large towns and cities along the Western Front, and few civilians died in the fighting. Unfortunately, hundreds of thousands of civilians died from starvation, because there were terrible food shortages during the war.

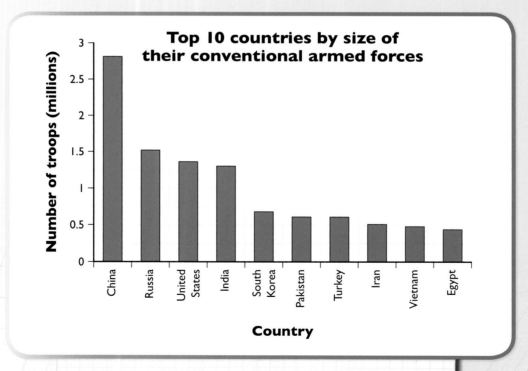

This bar graph shows the 10 countries with the largest conventional armed forces.

During World War II, the fighting did not avoid cities. Air forces on both sides dropped bombs on towns and cities deep inside enemy territory. These bombing raids killed many civilians. There were also fierce battles in some large cities, such as Stalingrad in Russia. The city was first attacked by **artillery** (heavy guns), which killed many civilians.

Recent conventional wars

Since World War II there have been a number of conventional wars, including the Korean War (1950–1953), the Iran–Iraq War (1980–1988), and the wars between India and Pakistan in 1947, 1965, and 1971. However, conventional wars have become much less common in recent years.

 During World War II, there was large-scale bombing of civilian targets for the first time. Coventry Cathedral, in the United Kingdom, was virtually destroyed in a huge air raid in 1940.

CONVENTIONAL WEAPONS

There have been huge advances in conventional weapons since World War II. The technology behind many of these weapons was first developed during World War II.

Jets

Toward the end of World War II, both sides developed new aircraft powered by jet engines. They were faster than propeller planes, more powerful, and they could carry more weight. Early jets could fly fast, but they could not fly long distances and were not very agile. By the 1960s, jet fighters and bombers were more agile and could fly faster than the speed of sound.

Early computers

Three of the earliest computers were built during World War II. In the United States, the ENIAC computer calculated tables that were used by gunners to aim artillery accurately. In the United Kingdom, the Colossus computer decoded secret German messages. The German Z-3 computer was built before either of these, but was destroyed in 1943 in a bomb attack on Berlin.

 This is the U.S. Air Force's newest stealth fighter. The electronics on board the Lockheed F-22 Raptor include a powerful radar system, a missile warning system, and computer-assisted flight controls.

Missiles

Near the end of World War II, Germany built the first missiles—the V-1 and the V-2. V-2 missiles were more accurate than V-1s, especially by the end of the war. They flew at a height of about 80 kilometers (50 miles) and fell on their target at four times the speed of sound. A V-2 could reach a target 240 kilometers (150 miles) away in less than 5 minutes.

After World War II, countries around the world began building missiles. Today, missiles are some of the most important weapons in military forces.

Electronics

Electronics and computers have improved weapons and military equipment. Electronic **guidance systems** have made missiles and other weapons more accurate. Computer-assisted flight controls have made it possible to build fighter aircraft that are very acrobatic. Electronic systems have also improved communications within modern fighting forces. Modern electronics can figure out exactly where an enemy aircraft is by detecting its **radar**. If the radar is turned off, a **Global Positioning System** (**GPS**) can locate the aircraft and guide missiles to hit them.

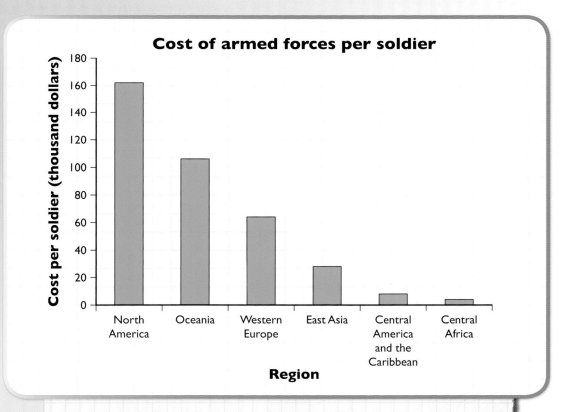

Cost of armed forces per soldier

(Bar graph — y-axis: Cost per soldier (thousand dollars), from 0 to 180; x-axis: Region)

- North America: ~162
- Oceania: ~106
- Western Europe: ~64
- East Asia: ~28
- Central America and the Caribbean: ~8
- Central Africa: ~4

Region

As the weapons the armed forces use become more advanced, the cost of equipping each soldier goes up. This bar graph shows how much money regions of the world spend on equipping their soldiers.

Any war involves many costs. The biggest cost is in human life. Hundreds, thousands, or even millions of people can be killed in a single war. Many others are injured, and often people are left with very serious injuries that will affect them for the rest of their lives.

Not all war casualties are due directly to fighting. In most wars, many civilians are also killed. In the past, the civilians killed in wars generally died from disease or because of food shortages caused by the war. In modern wars, civilians are more often killed by bombs, missiles, or other direct attacks.

Other costs

Wars also cause a great deal of property destruction. Homes, offices, factories, bridges, farm crops, and many other things are destroyed. After a war, land mines, unexploded bombs, and other dangerous equipment are left in the **war zone**. It can take many years to repair the destruction and remove hazards left behind.

Wars also cost a huge amount of money. In modern armed forces, all the troops have to be paid. Their weapons, warships, aircraft, and other military equipment all cost money to make. Producing and replacing military equipment can cost enormous amounts of money.

There can be casualties from a war long after the conflict has ended. Above, a doctor in Afghanistan aids a child who has lost both his legs in a land mine accident.

Geneva Conventions

In 1859 a young Swiss businessman named Henri Dunant was horrified to discover that many soldiers died on battlefields because there was no one there who could treat their wounds. In 1864 he organized a conference that wrote a set of rules about how wounded soldiers should be treated. By 1867 most European countries had agreed to stick by these rules.

The 1864 rules were the first version of what are now called the Geneva Conventions. The latest Geneva Conventions include other rules—for instance, stating how prisoners of war should be treated. Today, 194 countries have agreed to follow the Geneva Conventions.

Ethnic cleansing

This split bar graph shows casualties in the Bosnian War (1992–1995). The Bosnian War was a complex civil war between various groups of people who were all previously part of the country of Yugoslavia. The group that suffered the biggest casualties was the Bosnians. Serb soldiers killed thousands of Bosnian civilians in an attempt to completely wipe out the Bosnian people (ethnic cleansing).

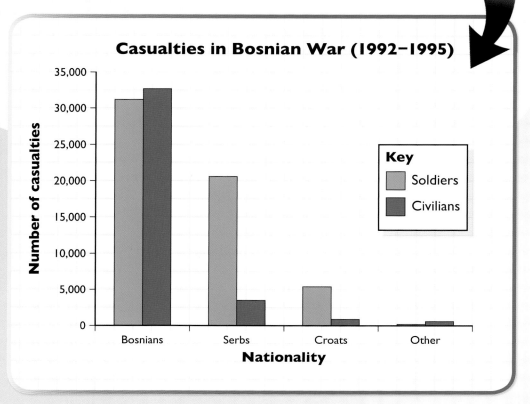

Casualties in Bosnian War (1992–1995)

Key: Soldiers, Civilians

Number of casualties (y-axis: 0 to 35,000)

Nationality (x-axis: Bosnians, Serbs, Croats, Other)

In August 1945, the United States dropped two enormously powerful bombs on Japan. The first was dropped on the city of Hiroshima, and it killed about 120,000 people. The second bomb landed on the city of Nagasaki. It killed around 80,000 people. Most of the people killed by both bombs were civilians.

Mass destruction

The bombs dropped on Hiroshima and Nagasaki were the first nuclear weapons. After World War II, the United States and the **Soviet Union** quickly developed more powerful nuclear weapons. In 1952 a much more powerful nuclear bomb, called the hydrogen bomb, was first tested. It was over 1,000 times more powerful than the first nuclear bombs.

Soon nuclear weapons were combined with rocket-powered missiles. By the 1960s, the United States, Soviet Union, United Kingdom, France, and China all had nuclear missiles that could be fired at any part of the world.

 This huge mushroom cloud is from a nuclear test explosion in the Nevada Desert in 1953. As the dangers of nuclear explosions became better understood, nuclear tests were carried out underground, to minimize the release of radiation. Today, most countries do not carry out test explosions at all.

Radiation hazard

Only part of the damage done by a nuclear weapon is caused by the explosion itself. A nuclear weapon also produces large amounts of nuclear radiation when it explodes. Large amounts of nuclear radiation can kill people. Lower amounts can make people very sick. The radiation from a nuclear explosion can spread over a large area.

Changing war

The development of nuclear weapons has changed how wars are fought. By the 1960s several countries, in particular the United States and the Soviet Union, had enough nuclear weapons to destroy most of Earth. Nuclear powers no longer go to war with each other—it is too dangerous. If either side used nuclear weapons, the other side would do the same. With such powerful weapons, both countries would be destroyed.

Nuclear treaties

For most of the time since World War II, there was an "arms race" between the United States and the Soviet Union. Both countries built more and more nuclear weapons in order to keep up with the other side. From the 1970s on, the United States and Russia signed several **treaties** (agreements), in which they agreed to limit the number of new nuclear weapons they would build.

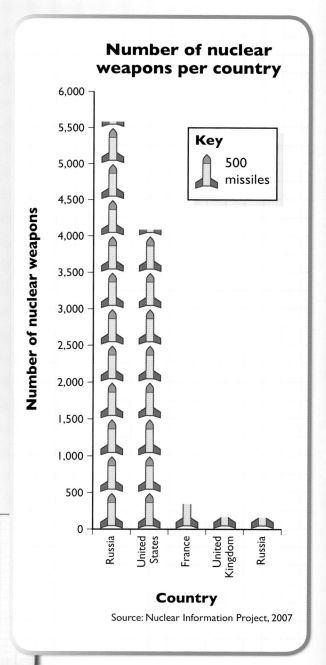

Source: Nuclear Information Project, 2007

 This pictogram shows some of the countries that currently hold nuclear weapons. Two major countries not shown that also hold nuclear weapons are North Korea and Israel.

CIVIL WAR

There have been far fewer conventional wars since World War II. Sadly, this does not mean that people are no longer fighting. What has happened is that different kinds of warfare have become important. Some of the most terrible and drawn-out wars that have happened since World War II have been civil wars.

What is a civil war?

A civil war is one in which two groups within the same country go to war with each other.

Many recent civil wars have taken place in countries that were once **colonized** by a European power. In the 1950s and 1960s, many of these colonies became independent countries. Often, different groups fought each other to take control of the new country.

The Vietnam War is an example of a civil war in a former colony. Until 1954, Vietnam was part of the French colony of Indochina. This area was split into three countries—Laos, Cambodia, and Vietnam.

U.S. soldiers in camouflage patrol during the Vietnam War. Many parts of Vietnam were heavily forested, which made it hard for conventional troops to fight guerrillas.

During fighting in the 1950s, Vietnam became split into North Vietnam, ruled by a communist government, and South Vietnam, governed by an elected president and a prime minister. North and South fought each other for control of the whole country. North Vietnam was supported by the communist governments of China and the Soviet Union, while South Vietnam was supported by the United States.

In 1965 the United States sent troops to fight for South Vietnam. U.S. forces stayed in Vietnam until 1973. In 1975 the whole country came under communist rule. During the war, at least 1.5 million people were killed. The fighting also spread to Laos and Cambodia, where millions more people died.

Timeline of major civil wars

Below is a timeline of some of the major civil wars since 1945, when World War II ended. Many of the worst wars since 1945 have been civil wars. In the conflicts in Sudan and Rwanda, for example, millions of people were killed—many of them defenseless civilians.

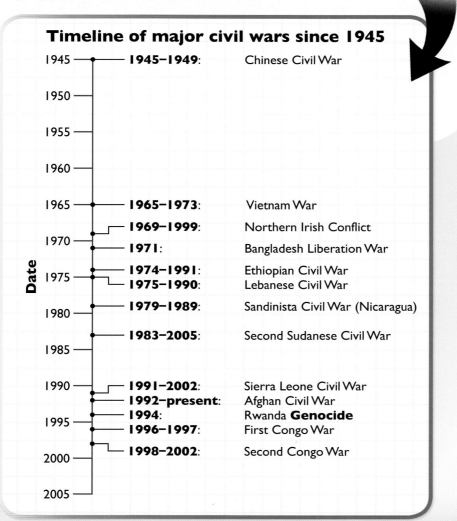

Timeline of major civil wars since 1945

Date		
1945	**1945–1949**:	Chinese Civil War
1965	**1965–1973**:	Vietnam War
	1969–1999:	Northern Irish Conflict
1970	**1971**:	Bangladesh Liberation War
1975	**1974–1991**:	Ethiopian Civil War
	1975–1990:	Lebanese Civil War
	1979–1989:	Sandinista Civil War (Nicaragua)
	1983–2005:	Second Sudanese Civil War
1990	**1991–2002**:	Sierra Leone Civil War
	1992–present:	Afghan Civil War
	1994:	Rwanda **Genocide**
	1996–1997:	First Congo War
	1998–2002:	Second Congo War

GUERRILLA WAR

Guerrilla fighting is a kind of warfare that is often used when one side in a war has a much bigger conventional army than the other. The side with the small army uses small bands of fighters to make focused attacks on the enemy.

Many of the wars that have happened since World War II have involved guerilla warfare. In the Vietnam War, for example, a group of fighters called the Viet Cong fought a guerrilla war against U.S. and South Vietnamese soldiers, with support from the regular North Vietnamese army.

Guerrilla fighting is also used in civil wars. In the 1970s, the country of Nicaragua was ruled by a **dictator**, President Anastasio Somoza. Fighters called Sandinistas, who wanted to get rid of Somoza, used guerrilla tactics to try to remove him. In 1979 they were successful.

 A female fighter holds a weapon in Mogadishu, Somalia, in 2009. Somalia has not had a real government since President Siad Barre was overthrown in 1991. The country is run by warlords who are always in conflict with each other.

Guerrilla tactics

Guerrilla fighters usually work in small groups. They find out about the enemy and look for weak points where they can attack. Then they strike hard and leave quickly.

Guerrillas attack various kinds of targets. They might **ambush** a small group of troops or destroy a bridge, a building, an airfield, or some other target. They might try to **assassinate** an important enemy general or leader, or even local leaders and teachers. They may also disrupt communications or spread false information.

Being able to act quickly and move quickly is essential for guerrilla forces. They rarely have a headquarters or a base, but they do need places where they can hide safely after an attack. Guerrillas often hide out in forests or mountainous areas. They can also disappear in cities, simply by mixing with the general population.

Supplies and weapons

Guerrilla fighters are often **insurgents**—they are fighting to get rid of the government. Insurgents often get support from the rest of the population, who may agree with their aims. They may also get support from other countries. In the Northern Ireland conflict, the Irish Republican Army (IRA) fought a guerrilla war against the British army. They received money and support from Catholics within Northern Ireland, and from Irish-Americans in the United States.

The first guerrillas

Between 1808 and 1814, the French armies of Napoleon fought the Peninsular War to try to take control of Spain and Portugal. The French defeated the Spanish army in battle. However, small groups of Spanish fighters continued to fight the French by launching surprise attacks and stopping communications. The Spanish called this kind of fighting a *guerrilla*, which means "small war."

Terrorism

When small groups of fighters use bombs or other kinds of attack to deliberately kill or injure civilians, it is called terrorism rather than guerrilla warfare. Terrorists use similar tactics to guerrilla fighters. However, their attacks are often deliberately designed to frighten people or governments. Terrorists may **kidnap** important people or their families. They may hijack (take over by force) aircraft, or plant bombs in crowded city centers. They may also carry out **suicide bombings** or gas attacks.

Ancient terrorism

Terrorist tactics have been used for thousands of years. The Chinese general Sun-Tzu wrote a book called *The Art of War* in about 350 BCE. One of the things he wrote was, "Kill one, frighten 10,000." The idea of frightening people through killing is at the heart of all terrorism.

 A fuel tanker burns in Baghdad, Iraq, in 2005, after a suicide bomber crashed his car into it.

Who are the terrorists?

In recent times, many terrorist groups have sprung up around the world. Most of them are based in a single country and fight for very specific aims. However, a few terrorist groups are international. The best known of these is Al-Qaeda, led by Osama Bin Laden. Al-Qaeda has carried out terrorist attacks against the United States and its allies (friendly countries) in many places around the world. The biggest of these attacks happened on September 11, 2001. Al-Qaeda terrorists hijacked airliners and crashed them into the World Trade Center, in New York City, and the Pentagon, in Washington, D.C. Nearly 3,000 people were killed. A series of Al-Qaeda bombings on trains in Madrid, Spain, killed nearly 200 people in 2004, and there was a similar set of bombings in London, England, in 2005.

Terrorism, 1995–2003

The line graph below shows the numbers of terrorist attacks each year from 1995 to 2003 (in red). It also shows the number of people killed in these attacks (in blue). The large peak in 2001 is due to the thousands of people who were killed in the September 11 terrorist attacks in the United States.

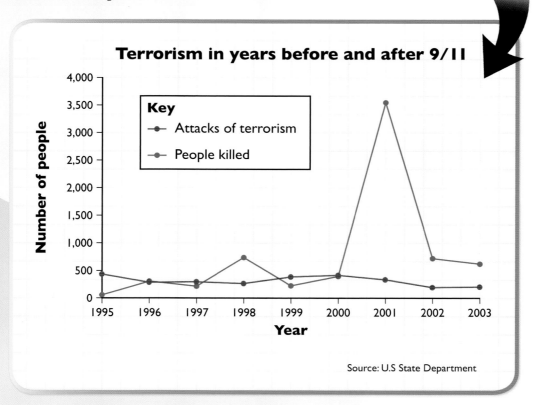

Terrorism in years before and after 9/11

Key
- Attacks of terrorism
- People killed

Number of people

Year

Source: U.S State Department

MODERN ARMED FORCES

Armed forces have had to adapt to fit in with the new kinds of warfare. A modern fighting force has to be able to work in many different situations. For example, it could be involved in full-scale warfare, **peacekeeping**, or disaster relief.

Small and flexible

Modern armed forces generally work in smaller units than in the past. Partly this is because of developments in technology. A small army patrol unit today is far more effective than it would have been in the past. Today, they can carry more weapons and fire them more quickly. And with modern communications, they can quickly call up **air support**. Small units also work best for many of the jobs that the armed forces have to do.

Below are some of the situations that modern armed forces might be involved in.

● *Border disputes*. Many countries have disagreements with neighboring countries about exactly where their borders are. India, for example, has troops in Kashmir in the northwest, where it is in disagreement with Pakistan, and in the northeast, where it is in dispute with China.

● *Insurgency or terrorism*. Armed forces often have to deal with terrorist attacks within their country (for example, if a terrorist group takes hostages). They may also have to combat insurgents. France and Spain have troops in the Basque region on the Spanish–French border. The troops are there to oppose Basque separatists, who want this region to be an independent country.

● *Peacekeeping forces*. The **United Nations** (UN) uses troops from the armies of many countries to help keep the peace in areas where people have recently been at war. For example, one of the largest peacekeeping forces is a UN force known as UNAMID. This force is based in the Darfur region of Sudan, in north Africa. Its job is to protect **refugees**—people who fled from their homes during a long-running civil war in Sudan.

● *Occupation*. When an armed force invades a country and defeats its armies, the invaders then take over the running of the country for a time. An armed force from the United States and allied countries invaded Iraq in 2003 and took over the country. Iraq now has its own government, but there are still large numbers of U.S. troops there. Their aims are to stop further fighting and to train local fighting forces to take over security.

Disaster relief

Military forces can play an extremely important role during disasters such as floods, earthquakes, or hurricanes. In 2005 a powerful earthquake hit northern Pakistan. Over 86,000 people were killed, and around 4 million people lost their homes. Military forces from many countries helped with the relief effort. The Pakistan Army provided thousands of soldiers and engineers to help rescue people from fallen buildings and to provide people with food and shelter. They were supported by military teams from many other countries. The U.S. military, for example, provided large numbers of helicopters for moving people and supplies.

 In 2008 a terrible earthquake hit China's Sichuan province, killing nearly 70,000 people. Chinese military forces played a very important part in the huge disaster relief operation.

Intelligence

In many situations, modern armed forces are fighting against enemies that are hard to identify. Terrorists and insurgents, for example, do not wear uniforms and do not fight in large, organized groups. In these situations, **intelligence** is as important as weapons and transportation.

Intelligence is information. Some intelligence can come from satellites in space, or high-speed **reconnaissance** aircraft. They can detect training camps, weapons stores, and other information. Gathering intelligence also involves work on the ground, questioning people and learning about the aims and beliefs of the insurgents.

UN peacekeeping operations

As this pie chart below shows, military forces play a major part in United Nations (UN) peacekeeping operations worldwide. Smaller numbers of police and civilians are also involved in peacekeeping missions. The UN does not have its own army. Soldiers from many different countries make up UN peacekeeping forces.

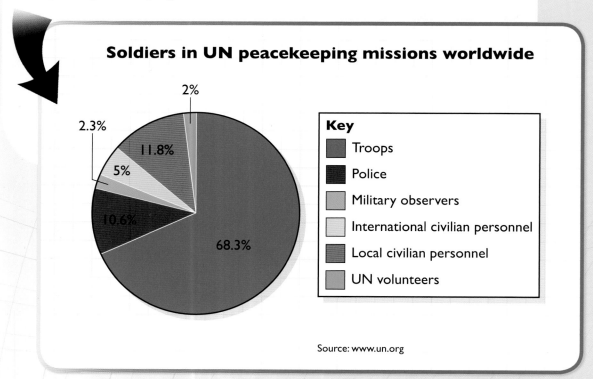

Soldiers in UN peacekeeping missions worldwide

2%
2.3%
11.8%
5%
10.6%
68.3%

Key
- Troops
- Police
- Military observers
- International civilian personnel
- Local civilian personnel
- UN volunteers

Source: www.un.org

 This photo shows the Iranian Embassy Siege in London in 1980. British special forces rescued hostages from terrorists who had broken into the embassy.

Special forces rescue

Special forces have become increasingly important in modern armed forces. These are highly trained, carefully chosen troops that work in small units. Special forces try to keep their operations secret. However, in 1980, the British special forces, called the SAS, were involved in a very public operation in the full view of news crews and television cameras. A group of six terrorists broke into the Iranian Embassy in London and took 26 people hostage. After several days of negotiations, the terrorists killed a hostage. Twenty minutes later, SAS soldiers burst into the embassy, rescued the hostages, and killed all but one of the terrorists. One more hostage was killed during the rescue.

THE CHANGING FACE OF WAR

This book has shown how wars have changed since 1945, when World War II ended. New technology and improved weapons have given armed forces far more destructive power and made them much more mobile. Nuclear weapons, first used at the end of World War II, are so destructive that military forces have not used them for over 60 years.

Less conventional

This book has also shown how conventional war has become less common, but other kinds of warfare have taken its place. Armed forces have become involved in civil wars, guerrilla wars, wars with insurgents, anti-terrorism, and peacekeeping operations.

 Being a soldier in a modern army is a complex and demanding job. At different times soldiers have to be peacekeepers, relief workers, guerrillas, and street fighters.

Blurring the boundaries

In conventional war it is clear who the enemy forces are, and soldiers and civilians are easy to tell apart. In many wars today, these boundaries are much less clear. This blurring of the boundaries makes it very important for armed forces to have good intelligence. Without this, they cannot clearly identify and target the enemy.

Fighting for a reason

No one likes wars. But most people support their armed forces. Soldiers are not the people who start wars. But they take all the risks. When they are fighting, their lives are in danger. They go to war to protect their friends, their relatives, and their homes. Wars are horrible, not heroic. But sometimes the soldiers fighting can be heroes.

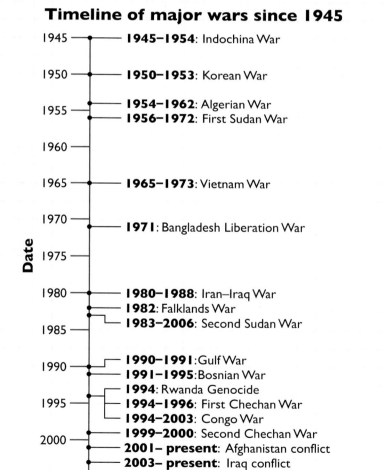

Timeline of major wars since 1945

Date

- 1945 — **1945–1954**: Indochina War
- 1950 — **1950–1953**: Korean War
- 1955 — **1954–1962**: Algerian War
  1956–1972: First Sudan War
- 1960 —
- 1965 — **1965–1973**: Vietnam War
- 1970 — **1971**: Bangladesh Liberation War
- 1975 —
- 1980 — **1980–1988**: Iran–Iraq War
  1982: Falklands War
  1983–2006: Second Sudan War
- 1985 —
- 1990 — **1990–1991**: Gulf War
  1991–1995: Bosnian War
  1994: Rwanda Genocide
- 1995 — **1994–1996**: First Chechan War
  1994–2003: Congo War
  1999–2000: Second Chechan War
- 2000 — **2001– present**: Afghanistan conflict
  2003– present: Iraq conflict
- 2005 —

 This timeline shows some of the major wars that have happened around the world since the end of World War II in 1945.

CHART SMARTS

Data is information about something. We often get important data as a mass of numbers, and it is difficult to make any sense of them. Graphs and charts are ways of displaying data visually. This helps us to see relationships and patterns in the numbers. Different types of graphs or charts are good for displaying different types of information.

Bar graphs

Bar graphs are a good way to compare amounts of different things. Bar graphs have a vertical **y-axis** showing the **scale**, and a horizontal **x-axis** showing the different types of information.

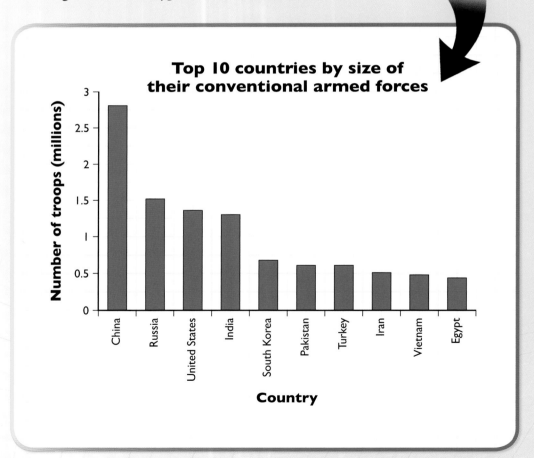

Pie charts

A pie chart is the best way to show how something is divided up. Pie charts show information as different-sized portions of a circle or slices of a "pie." They can help you compare proportions. You can easily see which section is the largest slice of the whole pie.

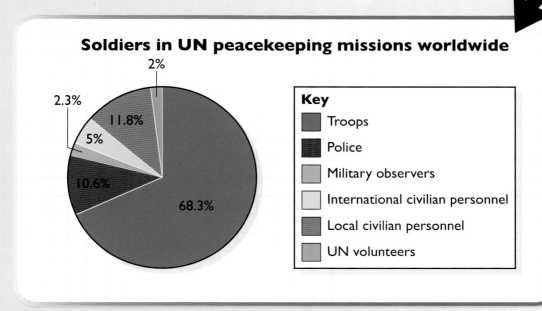

Soldiers in UN peacekeeping missions worldwide

2%
2.3%
11.8%
5%
10.6%
68.3%

Key
- Troops
- Police
- Military observers
- International civilian personnel
- Local civilian personnel
- UN volunteers

Line graphs

Line graphs use lines to join up points on a graph. They can be used to show how something changes over time. If you put several lines on one line graph, you can compare the overall pattern of several sets of data. Time is usually shown on the **x-axis**.

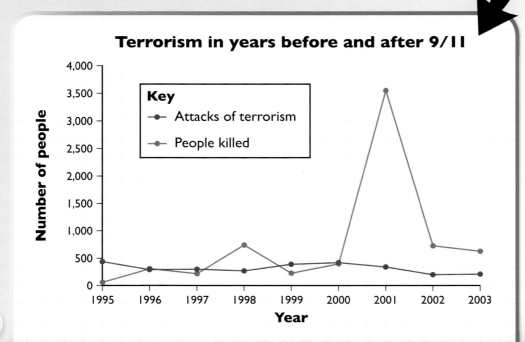

Terrorism in years before and after 9/11

Key
- Attacks of terrorism
- People killed

Number of people (y-axis: 0, 500, 1,000, 1,500, 2,000, 2,500, 3,000, 3,500, 4,000)

Year (x-axis: 1995, 1996, 1997, 1998, 1999, 2000, 2001, 2002, 2003)

GLOSSARY

air support aircraft helping troops on the ground by firing on enemy ground troops or other aircraft

ambush surprise attack

armed forces army, navy, and air force

artillery large, heavy guns that fire explosive shells

assassinate kill a leader or important person

casualty person killed or injured

civilian person not belonging to the armed forces or fighting in the war

colonized when a country been taken over and is being run by another country

conflict disagreement

conventional warfare way that wars have generally been fought in the past, between two armies on a battleground

dictator ruler who controls everything in a country

division large army unit of 10,000 to 20,000 soldiers

fortified protected by walls, trenches, or other defenses

genocide destruction of a group of people

Global Positioning System (GPS) system of satellites orbiting Earth that can pinpoint any position on Earth within a few feet

guidance system combination of electronics and sensors (instruments that measure things such as gravity or distance) that is used to guide a missile to its target

insurgent person who is fighting to get rid of his or her own country's government

intelligence information about the enemy's movements or plans

kidnap take someone prisoner and demand money or something else in exchange for his or her release

peacekeeping when armed forces are used to prevent fighting between groups that have been at war

radar (Radio Detection And Ranging) system for "seeing" aircraft or other objects at night, in fog, or from a distance

reconnaissance exploring or surveying in order to get intelligence

refugee person who has been forced out of his or her home and off his or her land by war or violence

scales numbered lines on a graph or chart

Soviet Union large country that was made up of Russia, Ukraine, and other areas that are now independent countries. The Soviet Union broke up in 1991.

suicide bombing when a terrorist straps explosives to his or her body and then blows himself or herself up, killing other people at the same time

treaty agreement between two or more countries

trench long, narrow hole in the ground used for fighting

United Nations organization representing all the countries of the world, which works for peace, unity, better health, and better living conditions for all people

x-axis horizontal axis of a graph or chart

y-axis vertical axis of a graph or chart

war zone area where a battle has taken place

FURTHER INFORMATION

Books

Adams, Simon. *World War I (Eyewitness)*. New York: Dorling Kindersley, 2007.

Adams, Simon. *World War II (Eyewitness)*. New York: Dorling Kindersley, 2007.

Davis, Barbara J. *One Million Lost: The Battle of the Somme*. Mankato, Minn.: Capstone, 2009.

Downing, David. *The War in Iraq (Witness to History)*. Chicago: Heinemann Library, 2004.

English, June. *Scholastic Encyclopedia of the United States at War*. New York: Scholastic: 2003.

Fitzgerald, Brian. *Fighting the Vietnam (War on the Front Line)*. Chicago: Raintree, 2006.

Websites

Learn more about the Vietnam War at this site sponsored by the Public Broadcasting Service (PBS).
www.pbs.org/battlefieldvietnam/

Find out more about World War I at this PBS site, which includes a glossary, timeline, and more.
www.pbs.org/greatwar/

You can learn more about World War II at this PBS site. Explore an interactive timeline, read letters from people who experienced the war, and view a large collection of photos and video clips.
www.pbs.org/perilousfight/

Learn about the Iraq War at this site, sponsored by Time Magazine for Kids. You will get to read different perspectives on the war, view maps, read a timeline of the conflict, and more.
www.timeforkids.com/TFK/specials/iraq/0,8805,424876,00.html

INDEX